WORLD HISTORY
THE HUMAN EXPERIENCE

Skill Reinforcement Activities

Mounir A. Farah

Andrea Berens Karls

GLENCOE
McGraw-Hill

New York, New York   Columbus, Ohio   Woodland Hills, California   Peoria, Illinois

Customize Your Resources

No matter how you organize your teaching resources, Glencoe has what you need.

The **Teacher's Classroom Resources** for *World History: The Human Experience* provides you with a wide variety of supplemental materials to enhance the classroom experience. These resources appear as individual booklets accompanied by a file management kit of file folders, labels, and tabbed binder dividers in a carryall file box. The booklets are designed to open flat so that pages can be easily photocopied without removing them from their booklets. However, if you choose to create separate files, the pages are perforated for easy removal. You may customize these materials using our file folders or tabbed dividers.

The individual booklets and the file management kit supplied in **Teacher's Classroom Resources** give you the flexibility to organize these resources in a combination that best suits your teaching style. Below are several alternatives:

- **Organize all resources by category**
  (all Tests, all Geography and History Activities, all History Simulations, and so on, filed separately)

- **Organize resources by category and chapter**
  (all Chapter 1 activities, all Chapter 1 tests, etc.)

- **Organize resources sequentially by lesson**
  (activities, quizzes, study guides, etc., for Section 1, Section 2, and so on)

Glencoe/McGraw-Hill
A Division of The McGraw·Hill Companies

Copyright © by The McGraw-Hill Companies, Inc. All rights reserved. Permission is granted to reproduce the material contained herein on the condition that such material be reproduced only for classroom use; be provided to students, teachers, and families without charge; and be used solely in conjunction with *World History: The Human Experience.* Any other reproduction, for use or sale, is prohibited without prior written permission of the publisher.

Send all inquiries to:
Glencoe/McGraw-Hill
936 Eastwind Drive
Westerville, OH 43081

ISBN 0-02-821588-5

Printed in the United States of America
2 3 4 5 6 7 8 9 10 045 03 02 01 00 99

SKILL REINFORCEMENT ACTIVITIES

TABLE OF CONTENTS

To the Teacher		iv
Chapter 1	Understanding Map Projections	1
Chapter 2	Classifying Information	2
Chapter 3	Problem Solving	3
Chapter 4	Making Comparisons	4
Chapter 5	Finding Exact Location on a Map	5
Chapter 6	Decision Making	6
Chapter 7	Interpreting Point of View	7
Chapter 8	Determining Cause and Effect	8
Chapter 9	Identifying Central Issues	9
Chapter 10	Distinguishing Between Fact and Opinion	10
Chapter 11	Interpreting Demographic Data	11
Chapter 12	Making Inferences	12
Chapter 13	Analyzing Historical Maps	13
Chapter 14	Making Generalizations	14
Chapter 15	Analyzing Primary and Secondary Sources	15
Chapter 16	Identifying Evidence	16
Chapter 17	Using a Computerized Card Catalog	17
Chapter 18	Using a Word Processor	18
Chapter 19	Recognizing a Stereotype	19
Chapter 20	Developing Multimedia Presentations	20
Chapter 21	Outlining	21
Chapter 22	Interpreting Graphs	22
Chapter 23	Detecting Bias	23
Chapter 24	Using E-Mail	24
Chapter 25	Reading a Cartogram	25
Chapter 26	Selecting and Using Research Sources	26
Chapter 27	Using the Internet	27
Chapter 28	Interpreting Military Movements on Maps	28
Chapter 29	Analyzing Political Cartoons	29
Chapter 30	Identifying an Argument	30
Chapter 31	Synthesizing Information	31
Chapter 32	Understanding World Time Zones	32
Chapter 33	Using a Spreadsheet	33
Chapter 34	Writing a Research Report	34
Chapter 35	Preparing a Bibliography	35
Chapter 36	Developing a Database	36
Chapter 37	Interpreting Statistics	37
Answer Key		38
Acknowledgments		44

To the Teacher

Skill Reinforcement Activities pick up and extend the topic appearing on the Skills page of each chapter in *World History: The Human Experience.* There are four categories for this activity: Critical Thinking Skills, Social Studies Skills, Study and Writing Skills, and Technology Skills. The activities help students acquire and improve abilities essential to a historian—analyzing and interpreting maps, evaluating sources of information, and organizing and writing history.

Answers to the activities are provided at the back of the booklet.

Name .... Date .... Class ....

# SKILL REINFORCEMENT
Activity 1

Understanding Map Projections

Mapmakers, also called cartographers, use map projections to represent the earth's spherical surface on flat maps. Although extremely useful for study and navigation, flat maps cannot accurately represent both the shape and size of land areas. Cylindrical Projection (Mercator) maps like the one below give the directions and accurate shapes of areas of land and water, but they distort the size of land areas. The greater the distance between a land area and the Equator, the greater the distortion. Compare the diagram of a globe (or use a real globe, if possible) to the Cylindrical Projection map below. Then answer the questions that follow.

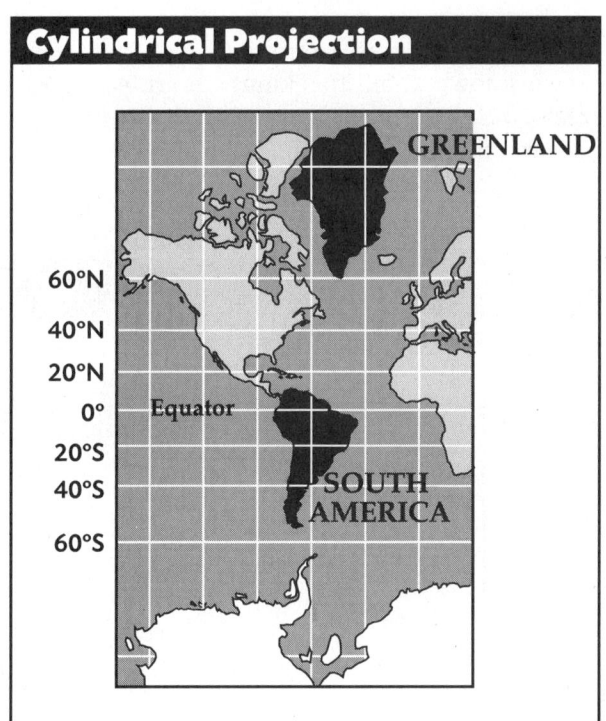

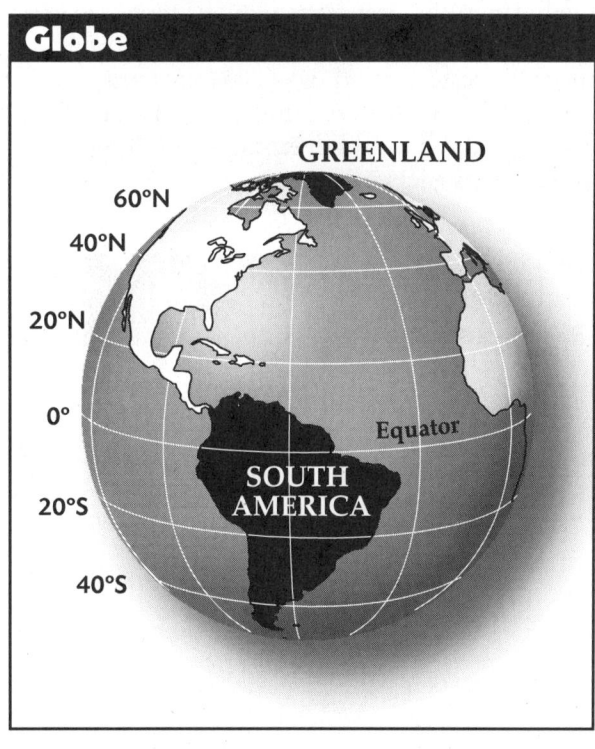

1. Without referring to the illustrations, which do you already know to be larger—South America or Greenland?
   _____

2. Which represents the relative sizes of South America and Greenland more accurately—the Cylindrical Projection map or the globe? Explain why.
   _____
   _____

3. Why are Cylindrical Projection maps particularly well suited for use in navigation?
   _____
   _____

World History   Skill Reinforcement Activities   1

Name .... Date .... Class ....

SKILL REINFORCEMENT Activity 2

Classifying Information

The following paragraphs tell about three of the kings of the Old Kingdom. As you read the selection, look for items that have similar characteristics. The chart below lists three categories of information. Add facts under the appropriate headings as you read.

King Djoser, who reigned from about 2737 to 2717 B.C., underscored national unity by including themes from both Upper and Lower Egypt in his tomb buildings. His architect used stone blocks instead of the traditional mud bricks, resulting in the first monumental stone structure in the world. The central element in the building, the Step Pyramid, was Djoser's tomb. Djoser developed an effective bureaucracy to handle the affairs of the central government and large construction projects.

King Snefru of the fourth dynasty built the first true pyramid at Dahshur. Snefru was a warrior who fought in Nubia, Libya, and the Sinai. He brought prosperity to the kingdom by promoting trade, mining, and shipbuilding.

Snefru was succeeded by his son, Cheops, who built the Great Pyramid at Giza. Not much else is known about this king, who ruled for 23 years, but the huge size and complexity of the construction project indicates how far the bureaucracy had advanced.

Kings of the Old Kingdom	Building	Other Accomplishments
Djoser		
Snefru		
Cheops		

Name .... Date .... Class ....

SKILL REINFORCEMENT Activity 3

Problem Solving

The problem-solving process can be used to understand why things happened in the past. By reading about an event, and then using your knowledge of the problem-solving process, you can begin to understand and explain why things happened as they did. Reread the information about the Israelite monarchy and the exile of the people of Israel and Judah on page 85 in your text. Use that information to complete the chart below. The first column has been done for you.

Identify the Problem	Gather Information	List the Options	List the Advantages & Disadvantages	Choose a Solution
continued warfare in Israel				

Now that you have completed the table, evaluate the effectiveness of the solution chosen by the people of Israel. Write a paragraph to explain why it was or was not an effective solution to the problem of warfare.

_____
_____
_____
_____
_____
_____
_____
_____

World History   Skill Reinforcement Activities   3

Name .... Date .... Class ....

SKILL REINFORCEMENT Activity 4

Making Comparisons

Remember that making comparisons means finding differences as well as similarities. Read the two passages below, which provide information about the Greek and Egyptian approaches to religion. Then complete the diagram to record what is unique to Greek religion and what is unique to Egyptian religion (differences), as well as what is common to both religions (similarities). Questions have been provided to help you start to organize the information on the chart.

Egyptian Religion

It is difficult to speak of Egyptian beliefs as religion, if "religion" means a unified system of belief. Although the most popular god was Ra, the god of the sun, every temple in Egypt worshiped its own local deities. The Egyptian gods and goddesses were pictured with human bodies and either animal or human heads. For example, Ra had a human body with the head of a hawk; like the hawk, the sun made its way swiftly across the sky. Anubis, a god connected with the dead, was given the head of a jackal because jackals were often found near desert graves. The Egyptians believed that after death the spirit, or ka, appeared before Osiris, lord of the dead. If the spirit was found to be just, it would go to a heavenly place called Yaru, where grain grew 12 feet high. If a person was evil, the ka would roam the world for eternity, continually hungry and thirsty.

Greek Religion

By the time Homer composed the *Iliad* and the *Odyssey* in the 700s B.C., the major gods and goddess of the Greeks had been well established, although each polis worshiped its own particular deity. The Greek deities were presented in an entirely human form but were given superhuman powers. For example, Poseidon controlled the seas and could cause violent storms at will. Like humans, the deities were subject to a force considered so powerful that not even Zeus could turn it back. This force was presented in the form of a goddess called Moira (Fate) or Ananke (Necessity). The Greeks also believed that humans possessed a soul that continued to live on after death. This soul would either remain on earth near the tomb of the deceased, hungrily waiting for funerary offerings, or it would depart to a dreary, shadowy region called Hades.

Questions

- How clearly organized were the Egyptian and Greek belief systems?
- What was the relationship between major gods and local temples?
- How were the physical forms of the gods and goddesses represented?
- What were the Egyptian and Greek concepts of the afterlife?

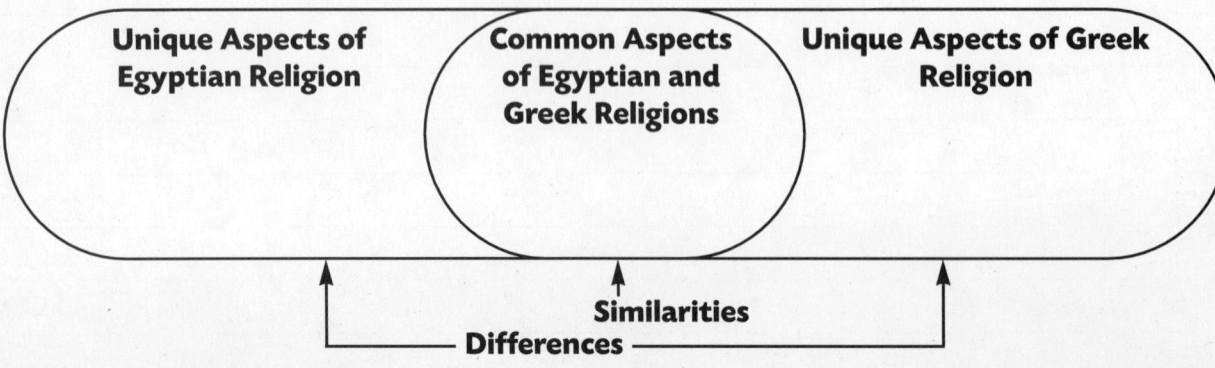

4 Skill Reinforcement Activities World History

Name .... Date .... Class ....

SKILL REINFORCEMENT
Activity 5

Finding Exact Location on a Map

By using the grid system of latitude and longitude lines, it is possible to locate any place on the earth. Lines of latitude measure the distance north and south of the equator, whereas lines of longitude measure the distance east and west of the Prime Meridian (0°longitude at Greenwich, England). Use the map below to answer the following questions. Estimate any grid values to the nearest tenth of a degree (for example, 40.2°N, 21.5°E).

The Greek Mainland

1. What is the approximate grid address of the following cities?

   a. Kalámai _____

   b. Thessaloniki _____

   c. Athens _____

2. What cities are located by the following grid addresses?

   a. 38.3°N, 21.7°E _____

   b. 39.4°N, 22.9°E _____

   c. 39.6°N, 19.9°E _____

World History   Skill Reinforcement Activities   5

Name _____ Date _____ Class _____

SKILL REINFORCEMENT
Activity 6

Decision Making

Many of the events you have studied in history occurred as a result of the decisions of groups or individuals. In many instances, people made decisions after considering alternatives, and then evaluating the consequences of those alternatives. In your own experience, taking time to identify alternatives and then considering the consequences allows you to make informed decisions.

Identify the alternatives, and describe their consequences for each of the following events that occurred during the time of ancient Rome. Use another sheet of paper if necessary.

1. Although the Romans drove out the Tarquins, skilled Etruscan artisans stayed on in Rome.

2. During his reign, Augustus introduced many reforms to the empire.

3. Tiberius proposed a law that limited the size of latifundia and redistributed land to the poor.

4. As conditions became more peaceful, Augustus reduced the size of the army.

5. The Romans built aqueducts throughout Europe.

6. From the A.D. 190s to the A.D. 280s, army legions installed many emperors, only to kill most of them off in rapid succession.

7. Christians believed that their religion was the only true faith and refused to honor the Roman emperor as a god.

8. After being named the emperor of Rome in A.D. 312, Constantine became a protector of Christianity.

9. Greek-speaking Christians in the East did not accept the authority of the pope over their churches.

10. Long after the collapse of the empire, Latin remained the written language of the Roman Catholic Church.

Name .... Date .... Class ....

SKILL REINFORCEMENT Activity 7

Interpreting Point of View

Knowing a person's point of view can help you think critically about what that person says. The excerpt below is from a book called *The Periplus of the Erythraean Sea,* which includes information about East African coastal trade. The excerpt was written about A.D. 60 by a Greek from the Roman Empire. He wrote the book to give Roman sailors information they would need in order to compete with Arab traders in East Africa. Read the excerpt, and answer the questions below.

The voyage to all these far-side [East African coastal] market-towns is made from Egypt about the month of July. . . . And ships are also customarily fitted out from . . . India, bringing to these far-side market-towns the products of their own places; wheat, rice, clarified butter, sesame oil, cotton cloth, . . . and girdles, and honey from the reed called *sacchari* [sugar]. Some make the voyage especially to these market-towns, and others exchange their cargoes while sailing along the [Arabian] coast. This country is not subject to a King, but each market-town is ruled by its separate chief. . . .

[After several days' journey] is the island of Menuthias [Pemba?], about three hundred stadia from the mainland, low wooded, in which there are rivers and many kinds of birds and the mountain-tortoise. There are no wild beasts except the crocodiles; but there they do not attack men. In this place there are sewed boats, and canoes hallowed from single logs, which they use for fishing and catching tortoise. In this island they also catch them in a peculiar way, in wicker baskets, which they fasten across the channel-opening between the breakers.

Two days' sail beyond, there lies the very last market-town . . . which is . . . Kilwa; in which there is ivory in great quantity, and tortoise-shell. Along this coast live men of piratical habits, very great in stature, and under separate chiefs for each place. The . . . chief governs it under some ancient right that subjects it to the sovereignty of the state that is become first in Arabia. And the people of Muza [in Arabia] now hold it . . . , and send thither many large ships; using Arab captains and agent, who are familiar with the natives and intermarry with them, and who know the whole coast and understand the language.

There are imported into these markets the lances made at Muza especially for this trade, and hatchets and daggers and awls, and various kinds of glass; and at some places a little wine, wheat, not for trade but to serve for getting the good-will of the savages. There are exported from these places a great quantity of ivory, . . . and rhinoceros-horn and tortoise-shell (which is in best demand after that from India), and a little palm-oil.

1. What is the general subject of the excerpt? _____

2. What do you know about the author that might reveal his point of view? _____

_____

3. What emotionally charged words and phrases indicate his point of view toward the people of East Africa? _____

_____

4. How does this author's point of view toward East African trade in early times compare and contrast with the description given in your textbook on pages 194–195? _____

_____

World History   Skill Reinforcement Activities   7

Name .... Date .... Class ....

SKILL REINFORCEMENT
Activity 8

Determining Cause and Effect

The establishment of cause-and-effect relationships is critical to understanding history. In fact, historians spend most of their time reviewing known facts and trying to determine some linkage between them. Here is your chance to be a historian. The facts below are not organized in any way. Your job is to compare each fact with what you already know about ancient India and then draw lines pairing the causes and their probable effects.

1. After the collapse of the Mauryan Empire, the northeastern, central, and southern regions of the Indian subcontinent became increasingly fragmented.

2. During the Gupta Empire, royal support was lavished on learning and the arts.

3. The simple social structure of the Aryans became complex as new peoples came under the rule of the rajahs.

4. Tribal princes, such as Siddhartha, searched for solutions to the same sort of problems tackled by teachers of the *Upanishads*.

5. The *Rig-Veda* states that the four varnas of Aryan society were: Brahmans, Kshatriyas, Vaisyas, and, last, Sudras.

6. The Gupta Empire reunified northern India, forming a Hindu state.

7. The carvings and paintings that can be seen on Ajanta's walls and ceilings show the fashions of the Gupta court.

8. The Buddha spent 45 years teaching the Four Noble Truths to his followers.

8   Skill Reinforcement Activities   World History

Name _____ Date _____ Class _____

SKILL REINFORCEMENT Activity 9

Identifying Central Issues

Finding the central issues in political speeches often presents a challenge. In part this happens because politicians must appeal to as broad a section of the population as possible. Read the speech below. It was given at the end of the Qin dynasty by Liu Chi, the man whose descendants would rule the mighty Han dynasty. To pick out the central issues he discusses, first identify his audience and whether they are happy or unhappy about their lives under the Qin. If they are unhappy, what do they want the Han to change, and how does the speech reflect those needs?

Gentlemen, for a long time you have suffered beneath the harsh laws of Ch'in [Qin]. Those who criticized the government were wiped out along with their families; those who gathered to talk in private were executed in the marketplace. I and the other lords have made an agreement that he who first enters the Pass shall rule over the area within. Accordingly I am now king of this territory of Kuan-chung. I hereby promise you a code of laws consisting of three articles only: 1) he who kills anyone shall suffer death; 2) he who wounds another or steals shall be punished according to the gravity of the offense; 3) for the rest I abolish all the laws of Ch'in [Qin]. Let the officials and people remain undisturbed as before. I have come only to save you from injury, not to exploit or oppress you. Therefore, do not be afraid!

1. What is Liu's main purpose in making this speech? How does he accomplish this purpose in his speech?
   _____
   _____

2. What Chinese social groups do you think Liu wants to influence by making this speech?
   _____
   _____

3. What aspects of Qin society does Liu believe have contributed to the suffering of the Chinese people under Shihuangdi?
   _____
   _____

4. From what you know of the Han dynasty, did Liu and his successors keep his promise "not to exploit or oppress" the people?
   _____
   _____

5. Imagine that you are a peasant listening to Liu's speech. On another sheet of paper, write a diary entry describing your feelings after the event took place. Be sure to include your reaction to Shihuangdi's laws and your hopes for Liu's dynasty.

World History   Skill Reinforcement Activities   **9**

Name .... Date .... Class ....

SKILL REINFORCEMENT
Activity 10

Distinguishing Between Fact and Opinion

Theodora, wife of Byzantine emperor Justinian I, was an unconventional woman—one who has attracted the attention of many historians and biographers. As questions about her life as an actress and then empress are debated, we hear a mixture of facts and opinions that attempt to explain her character and her importance in history. In order to evaluate these explanations, we must first know how to distinguish fact from opinion. Read the following passage, then answer the questions below.

The Woman Behind the Man Shows Her Strength

Byzantine emperor Justinian was a strong and well-educated leader. It is surprising that a man of such importance would have married an actress, no matter how beautiful she was. Yet Theodora was more than beautiful. She was intelligent and understood government. She influenced the awarding of some positions and generously gave jobs to friends.

Theodora also took action on behalf of women, convincing Justinian to grant a woman the right to own land that equaled the value of any wealth that she had brought to the marriage. It was only fair that a woman be no less wealthy after her marriage than she had been before it. Without this right to property, some widows had been unable to support their children.

Theodora's greatest achievement was saving her husband's position as emperor. During a rebellion, several of the emperor's advisers wanted to leave the city. Theodora announced that she would not leave. Justinian was able to suppress the rebellion and remain in power.

---

1. Does the title of the article express a fact or an opinion? Why?
   _____

2. **a.** List several facts from the article.
   _____
   _____

   b. How do you know these are facts?
   _____

3. Which individual words in this article suggest that an opinion is being expressed?
   _____

4. In a sentence or two, sum up the main opinion that the writer is expressing.
   _____
   _____

10   Skill Reinforcement Activities   World History

Name _____ Date _____ Class _____

SKILL REINFORCEMENT Activity 11

Interpreting Demographic Data

Demographic data are statistics about a population. The most commonly used demographic data tell the size of a population, or how many people there are. The graph below shows predicted population sizes for several countries. Examine the graph, then answer the questions that follow.

Title: _____

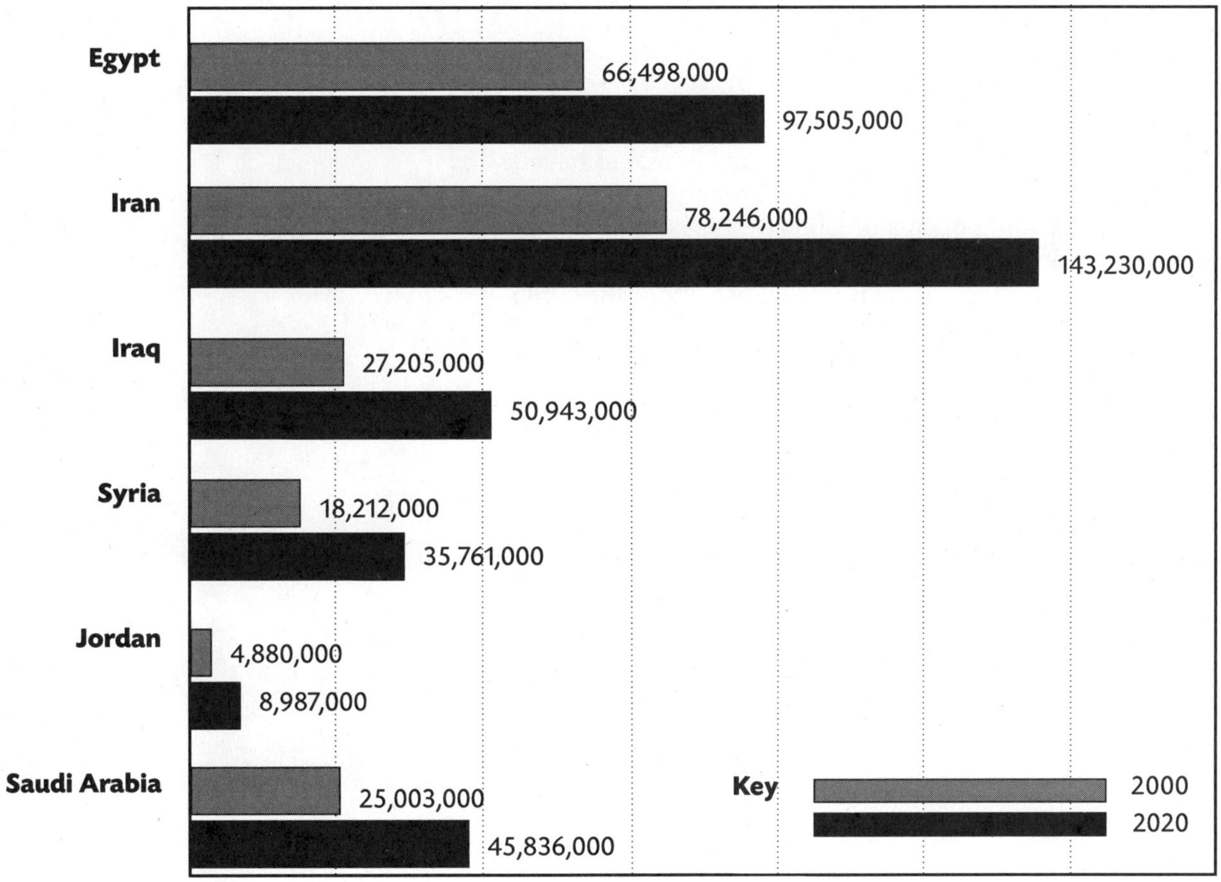

Egypt
- 66,498,000
- 97,505,000

Iran
- 78,246,000
- 143,230,000

Iraq
- 27,205,000
- 50,943,000

Syria
- 18,212,000
- 35,761,000

Jordan
- 4,880,000
- 8,987,000

Saudi Arabia
- 25,003,000
- 45,836,000

Key: 2000 / 2020

1. Write an appropriate title for the graph.
2. Which country will have the largest population by the year 2020? _____
3. Which country will have the smallest population by that year? _____
4. What is the predicted increase in the population of Syria between 2000 and 2020? About what percent of the population is this increase? _____
5. Which country is predicted to have the smallest rate of growth? _____
6. If Egypt grew at the rate of Syria, what would its population be in 2020? _____

World History   Skill Reinforcement Activities   **11**

Name .... Date .... Class ....

SKILL REINFORCEMENT Activity 12

Making Inferences

Few people in the Middle Ages could read or write. The small number of religious works and classical writings that were available had been laboriously copied by hand by the clergy. However, these medieval manuscripts were decorated with rich designs and intricate pictures. Contemporary scholars have often speculated about the purpose of the images appearing in the illuminated manuscripts. Look at the book page below and read the description that accompanies it. Then answer the questions that follow by making inferences about the purposes of each of the images.

Opening her *Book of Hours* [a book containing prayers] at Terce, the third canonical Hour of the day, which was at about 9 o'clock in the morning, a woman . . . would have seen herself on the 'dividing line' in the margin of the left-hand page. Holding open a tiny book—this book—she kneels before the Adoration of the Magi [the Bible story of three wise men who visit Jesus] that takes place under the triple arches of a Gothic shrine built into the letter 'D' of God's Word, *Deus*. Looking down to the *bas-de-page* [the base of the page], she would have seen how three monkeys ape the gestures of the wise men above. Top left, a spiky-winged ape-angel grasps the tail of the 'D,' as if he is about to pull the string that will unravel it all. Another simian plays a more supportive role, holding aloft, Atlas-like, the platform on which she kneels. On the sinister, or left side, and also mocking the gift-bearing Magi, struts a marvellous monster, known as a sciapod because of his one enormous foot, who proffers a golden crown.

From *Image on the Edge: The Margins of Medieval Art* by Michael Camille

Marguerite's *Monkey Business/Book of Hours*, British Library, London.

1. What inference can you make about the importance of Christianity to the woman reading this book?
   _____

2. What might be the reason for the three monkeys at the bottom of the page?
   _____

3. What might be the reason for the "spiky-winged ape-angel"?
   _____

4. What can you infer about the presence of the sciapod and the other grotesque figures?
   _____

12   Skill Reinforcement Activities   World History

SKILL REINFORCEMENT Activity 13

Analyzing Historical Maps

Analyzing historical maps can help you better understand where events occurred and their effects. Look at the map below of the Crusades, then answer the questions that follow.

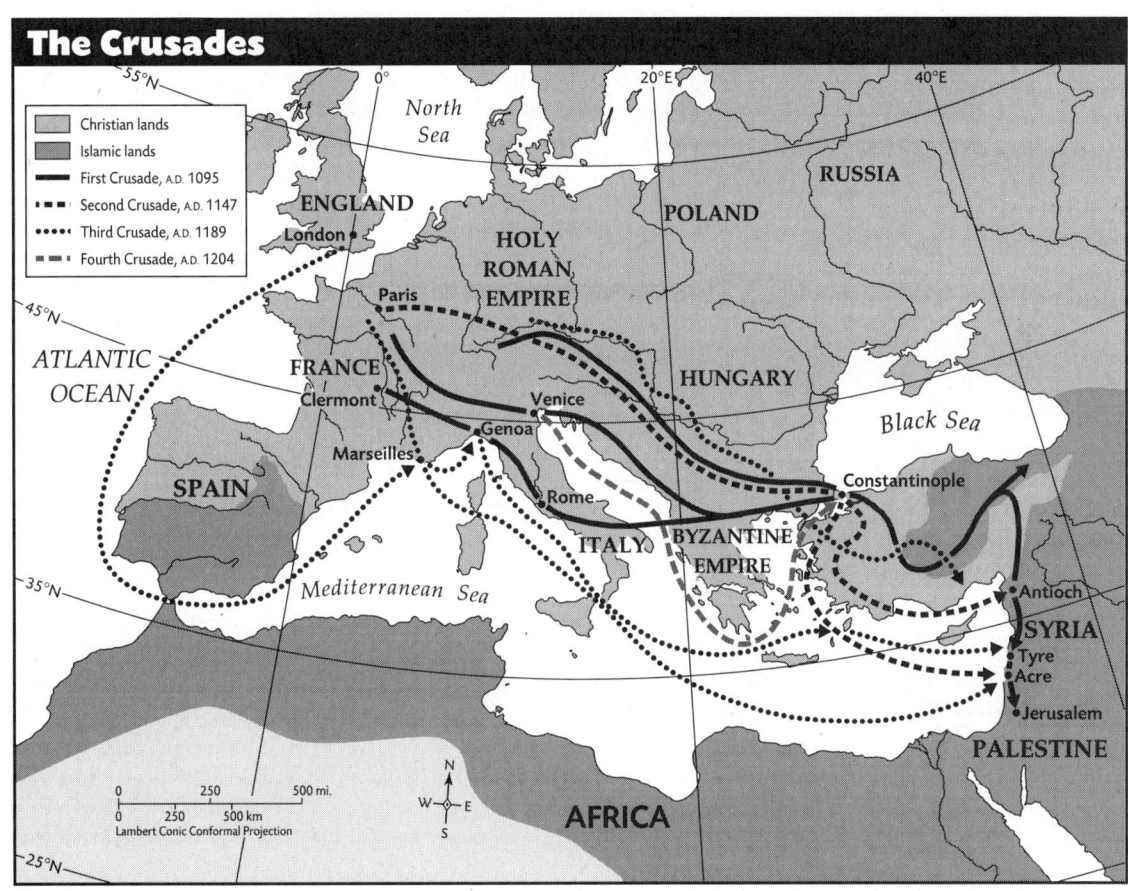

1. Which four time periods are shown on this map?

2. Look for the Crusaders who took the longest route to Jerusalem. Which Crusade was this? Where were they from? Through which cities did they pass to get to Jerusalem?

3. Describe the area on the map that is Christian.

4. Which areas are Islamic?

World History   Skill Reinforcement Activities   13

Name .... Date .... Class ....

SKILL REINFORCEMENT
Activity 14

Making Generalizations

Historians must be careful when they make generalizations based on observed data. They must back up each generalization they make with specific references to the sources they have used, so that others can trace the reasoning that went into making the generalization. A generalization made without reference to specific historical sources is usually viewed as an opinion and therefore not necessarily accurate. The passage below contains excerpts from the Japanese constitution prepared by the Japanese emperor Prince Shotoku. Read the passage and answer the questions that follow.

I. Harmony is to be valued, and an avoidance of wanton opposition to be honored. All men are influenced by partisanship, and there are few who are intelligent. Hence there are some who disobey their lords and fathers, or who maintain feuds with the neighboring villages. But when those above are harmonious and those below are friendly, and there is concord in the discussion of business, right views of things spontaneously gain acceptance. Then what is there which cannot be accomplished?

II. Sincerely reverence the three treasures. The three treasures, viz. Buddha, the Law, and the Monastic orders . . . are the supreme objects of faith in all countries. Few men are utterly bad. They may be taught to follow it. But if they do not betake them to the three treasures, wherewithal shall their crookedness be made straight?

III. When you receive the imperial commands, fail not scrupulously to obey them. The lord is Heaven, the vassal is Earth. Heaven overspreads, and Earth upbears. When this is so, the four seasons follow their due course, and the powers of Nature obtain their efficacy. If the Earth attempted to overspread, Heaven would simply fall in ruin. Therefore is it that when the lord speaks, the vassal listens; when the superior acts, the inferior yields compliance. Consequently when you receive the imperial commands, fail not to carry them out scrupulously. Let there be a want of care in this matter, and ruin is the natural consequence.

1. What statements are presented about Confucianism, Buddhism, and Chinese traditions in general? _____
_____
_____

2. What generalizations can you make based on these statements? _____
_____
_____

3. List the quotes from the document that support your generalizations. _____
_____
_____
_____

14   Skill Reinforcement Activities   World History

Name _____ Date _____ Class _____

SKILL REINFORCEMENT Activity 15

Analyzing Primary and Secondary Sources

Knowing the sources of information found in books and articles is critical to appraising their value as historical sources. Historians need a system to rate the accuracy of the information they collect. Read the following quotes, and determine which accurately represents the subject being discussed. The criteria to use in making your decisions should be: the type of source, who created it, when and where it was created, its topic, its purpose, and the source's reliability.

"The Spaniards had been allowed entry into the city so that they would learn to appreciate the extent of Moctezoma's [Montezuma's] greatness. Instead they seized him as hostage and puppet. As they clustered around him, gazing into his face, touching and prodding him, and then shackled him to teach him fear. His sacred power drained away."
—From *Aztecs: An Interpretation,* by historian Inga Clendinnen, 1991

"When our princes saw the great crowd that had formed there, they ordered that some should set about supplying open-air meals for them all, so that they should not be driven by hunger to disperse again across the heaths. Others were ordered to work on building huts and houses according to plans made by the Inca. Thus our imperial city began to be settled: it was divided into two halves called Hana Cuzco, which as you know, means upper Cuzco, and Hurin Cuzco, or lower Cuzco."
—From *Royal Commentaries of the Incas,* by Garcilaso de la Vega, El Inca, born in Peru in 1539 of Inca and Spanish ancestry. The book was first published in the 1600s and later translated by Harold V. Livermore

"Cicuye is a village of nearly five hundred warriors, who are feared throughout that country. The pueblo is square, situated on a rock, with a large courtyard in the middle containing underground council chambers. The houses are all alike, four stories high. One can go over the top of the whole village without a street to stop him. . . . The people of this village boast that no one has been able to conquer them and they conquer whatever villages they wish."
—From the journal of Pedro de Castañeda, a soldier in the army of Francisco de Coronado, 1560

"In 1531 Francisco Pizarro (ca. 1475–1541) matched Cortes' feat when he conquered the Peruvian empire of the Incas. This conquest vastly extended the territory under Spanish control and became the true source of profit for the crown, when a huge silver mine was discovered in 1545 at Potosí in what is now southern Bolivia. The gold and silver that poured into Spain in the next quarter century helped support Spanish dynastic ambitions in Europe."
—From *Civilizations in the West* by historians Mark Kishlansky, Patrick Geary, and Patricia O'Brien, 1991

1. Which of these sources qualify as primary sources? Secondary sources? Explain your answers.
_____
_____

2. What authority do the authors have? _____
_____

3. Do you think that materials which have been translated into another language qualify without a doubt as primary sources? Explain your answer. _____
_____

World History   Skill Reinforcement Activities   **15**

Name .... Date .... Class ....

SKILL REINFORCEMENT Activity 16

Identifying Evidence

Many Italians ventured north to further trade and share their learning among the Europeans. As they did so, many sent back letters and kept journals of their impressions. Read the following observations of life among the English by an Italian from about 1500, then answer the questions that follow.

. . . the English are great lovers of themselves, and of everything belonging to them; they think that there are no other men than themselves, and no other world but England; and whenever they see a handsome foreigner, they say that "he looks like an Englishman," and that "it is a great pity that he should not be an Englishman"; and when they partake of any delicacy with a foreigner, they ask him "whether such a thing is made in *their* country?" . . .

They have an antipathy to foreigners, and imagine that they never come into their island but to make themselves masters of it, and to usurp their goods; neither have they any sincere and solid friendships amongst themselves, insomuch that they do not trust each other to discuss either public or private affairs together, in the confidential manner we do in Italy.

—From *A Relation . . . of the Island of England*, trans. C.A. Sneyd

1. What evidence does the author offer to support the claim that the English people "are great lovers of themselves"?
_____
_____

2. What evidence does the author offer to support the claim that the English people "have an antipathy to foreigners"?
_____
_____

3. Which evidence do you find most convincing? Why?
_____
_____
_____

4. What do you think is the source for the evidence offered within the quotation marks? Is it primary or secondary evidence?
_____
_____

5. If this is a letter or diary, why must you be wary of its claims and evidence?
_____
_____

16   Skill Reinforcement Activities   World History

Name _____ Date _____ Class _____

SKILL REINFORCEMENT Activity 17

Using a Computerized Card Catalog

A computerized card catalog can help you find a specific book or a variety of resources about a research topic. Usually, you begin by requesting a particular kind of search, such as a title search, a search by author's name, or a search of materials on a general subject. Once you have located an item you want, you can check its call number, availability, or other information—such as date of publication for the source. If you requested a list of materials on the subject of slave trade, the screen display below might appear. Look through the materials as well as the information below the list. Then answer the questions that follow.

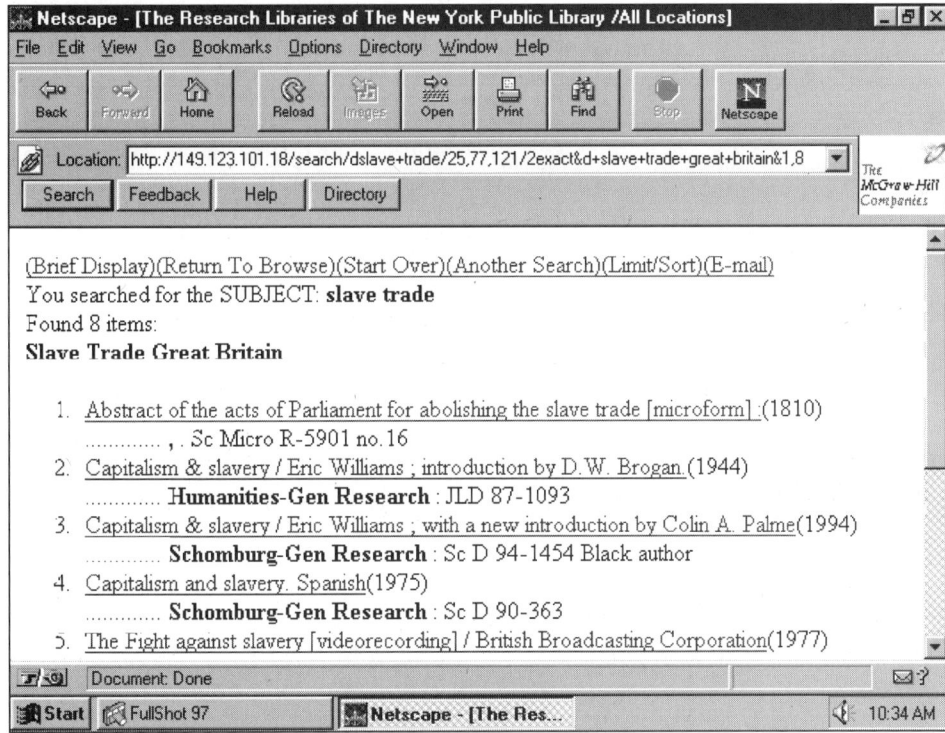

1. How many items in all are about Great Britain and the slave trade? _____
2. Which item is a video? _____
3. Which line would you click on to get information on a primary source? _____
4. In what part of the library would you find the most current edition of *Capitalism & Slavery*?

   _____

5. Which line would you click on to get information on a Spanish edition of the same book?

   _____

6. You have finished looking at books about the slave trade. What would you click on to find information about books on Dutch colonies in the Americas?

   _____

World History   Skill Reinforcement Activities   17

Name _____ Date _____ Class _____

SKILL REINFORCEMENT Activity 18

Using a Word Processor

A word processor can help you create a professional looking research paper. To make your research paper look professional, you will want to use many of the functions offered on your word processor. For example, you need to choose the font, the margins, and the line spacing. What other functions can you use on your word processor to get the look you want? Use a word processor to answer the following questions. If necessary, read your word processor user's manual, or click the Help button on the toolbar to help you.

1. What steps do you follow to set the margins of your document? _____
_____

2. How do you start a new paragraph? _____

3. How can a word be shown in boldface type? _____

4. What steps do you follow to show the page number on each page of your document? _____
_____

5. How would you center a title on your document? _____

6. Suppose you want to change the font of a title in your document. How would you do this?
_____
_____

7. What steps would you take to create a table with four columns and six rows? _____
_____

8. You are not finished with your research paper, but you must end your session on your computer. How do you save your work?
_____
_____

9. You have finished writing your research paper. How do you check for spelling errors?
_____
_____

10. You have proofread and looked over your research report on the word processor, and you're ready to print it. What steps do you take to print the document?
_____
_____

18   Skill Reinforcement Activities   World History

Name _____ Date _____ Class _____

 **SKILL REINFORCEMENT** Activity **19**

Recognizing A Stereotype

A stereotype is an oversimplified opinion, attitude, or judgment. It is a preconceived mental picture of a person or group. Stereotypes take advantage of the tendency people have to put all members of a particular group together without making distinctions between them as individuals. Although stereotypes can be positive or negative, they are usually negative. Have you heard stereotypes like these three examples?

    All cheerleaders are airheads.
    Old people are weak and foolish.
    City people are shrewd; country people are simple.

To create humor in his plays, William Shakespeare, the great dramatist of Elizabethan England, often took advantage of people's tendency to stereotype. Examples occur in the following passage from Act II, Scene ii of *Hamlet*. In this passage, Hamlet is using stereotypes to mock Polonius, the king's aged adviser. Read the passage and complete the chart to isolate and analyze the stereotypes in Hamlet's speech.

Polonius. What is the matter, my lord?
Hamlet. Between who?
Polonius. I mean the matter that you read, my lord.
Hamlet. Slanders, sir; for the satirical rogue says here that old men have grey beards, that their faces are wrinkled, their eyes purging thick amber and plum-tree gum, and that they have a plentiful lack of wit, together with most weak hams [legs]—all which, sir, though I most powerfully and potently believe, yet I hold it not honesty to have it thus set down, for yourself, sir, shall grow old as I am, if like a crab you could go backward.

Topic	Quote About Stereotype
Appearance	
Intelligence	
Physical Strength	

World History   Skill Reinforcement Activities   **19**

Name .... Date .... Class ....

SKILL REINFORCEMENT Activity 20

Developing Multimedia Presentations

Equipment you may have at home, as well as classroom or library resources, can make it possible for you to develop creative multimedia presentations. Most presentations are more interesting and can be easier to follow if they include diagrams, photographs, videos, or sound recordings.

Plan a multimedia presentation on a topic found in the chapter such as Isaac Newton's scientific discoveries, Ludwig van Beethoven's musical compositions, the Age of Enlightenment, or technology developed between 1750 and 1800. List three or four major ideas you would like to cover. Then think about how multimedia resources could enhance your presentation. Use the technology/media center to do a preliminary survey of materials that may be available, and list them on the chart. Use your imagination.

Topic: _____
Major Ideas: _____
_____
_____

Pictures, Posters, Photographs, Graphs, Diagrams, Charts	Videos	Animation	Sound Recordings

20   Skill Reinforcement Activities   World History

Skill Reinforcement Activity 21

Outlining

When taking notes as you read, it can be helpful to use an outline. Later, when you go back to the outline to study, the information will be organized and in a logical order. Complete the formal outline of Section 4 below.

I. The First Shot
    A. British march on Concord
    B. _____
    C. Minutemen fight at Lexington and Concord

II. _____
    A. Continental Congress
        1. Appoints George Washington commander
        2. _____
    B. *Common Sense*
        1. _____
        2. Helped convince Americans to separate from Great Britain
    C. _____
        1. Written by Thomas Jefferson
        2. Uses John Locke's idea of social contract

III. _____
    A. British Disadvantages
        1. _____
        2. _____
    B. _____
        1. George Washington's skill as general
        2. _____
    C. Turning Point and Conclusion
        1. Victory at Saratoga brings French into war
        2. _____

IV. Forming a New Government
    A. _____
        1. government could not collect taxes
        2. _____
        3. _____
    B. A New Constitution
        1. _____
        2. Three branches of central government
            a. _____
            b. _____
            c. _____
    C. _____
        1. Protected personal liberties
        2. _____

Name .... Date .... Class ....

SKILL REINFORCEMENT Activity 22

Interpreting Graphs

Graphs can show a great deal of information in a single, easy-to-read format. The graph below illustrates an important aspect of the situation in France just prior to the revolution. To interpret the graph, follow these steps: First, read the title. Then, read the captions and text. Finally, determine the relationships among all sections of the graph. When you have done so, use the graph to answer the questions that follow. Use a separate sheet of paper for your answers.

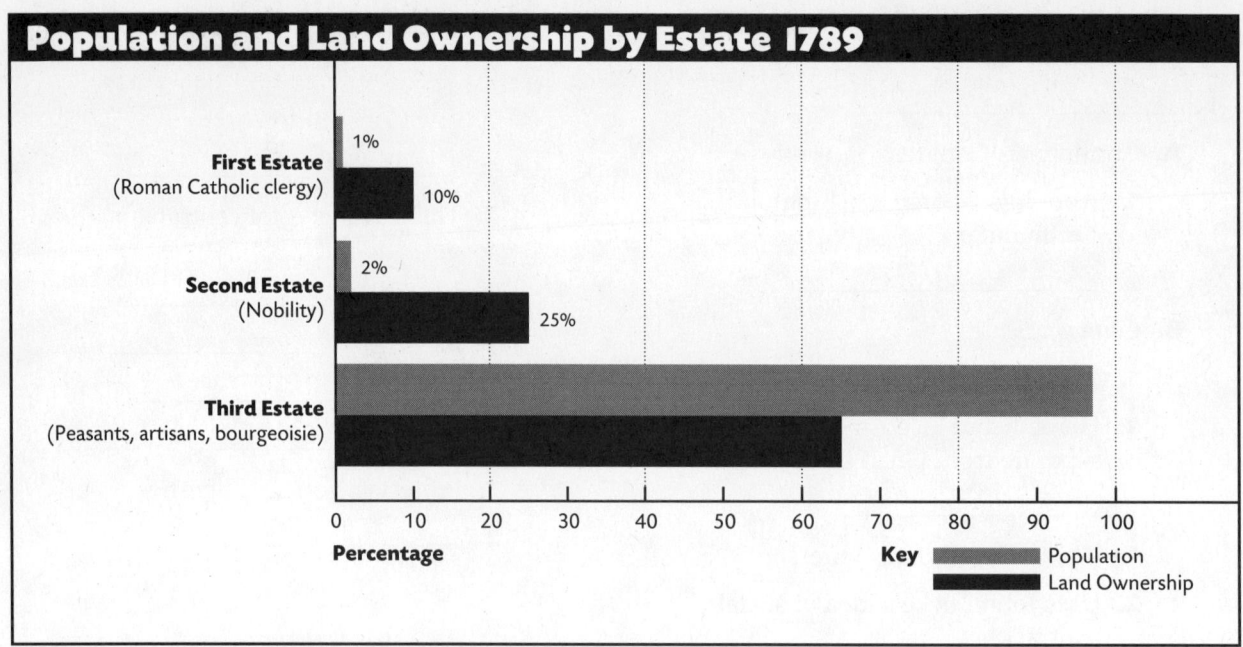

1. What does the horizontal axis of the graph represent?
2. **a.** What percentage of the French population comprised the First Estate?
   b. What percentage of land did they own?
3. **a.** What percentage of the French population comprised the Second Estate?
   b. What percentage of land did they own?
4. **a.** Calculate the percentage of the French population that comprised the Third Estate. Write the value on the graph.
   b. Calculate the percentage of land owned by the Third Estate. Write the value on the graph.
5. Why was land a good measure of wealth at this time?
6. Which estate had the greatest land ownership in proportion to its population?
7. **a.** How was the relationship between population and land ownership fundamentally different in the Third Estate?
   b. How might this fact have helped lead to the revolution?

22 Skill Reinforcement Activities   World History

Name _____ Date _____ Class _____

SKILL REINFORCEMENT Activity 23

Detecting Bias

Detecting bias can help you assess the accuracy of information that you read, hear, or view. Suppose you watch a television interview featuring several candidates for state or national office. By applying the skill of detecting bias, you can distinguish appeals for your support based on fact from appeals based on emotions. Read the following excerpt from American poet Walt Whitman's *Democratic Vistas*, published in 1871. Then answer the questions that follow.

In business (this all-devouring modern word, business,) the one sole object is, by any means, pecuniary [monetary] gain. The magician's serpent in the fable ate up all the other serpents; and money-making is our magician's serpent, remaining to-day sole master of the field. The best class we show, is but a mob of fashionably dress'd speculators and vulgarians. True, indeed, behind this fantastic farce, enacted on the visible stage of society, solid things and stupendous labors are to be discover'd, existing crudely and going on in the background, to advance and tell themselves in time. Yet the truths are none the less terrible. I say that our New World democracy, however great a success in uplifting the masses out of their sloughs, in materialistic development, products, and in a certain highly-deceptive superficial popular intellectuality, is, so far, an almost complete failure in its social aspects, and in really grand religious, moral, literary, and esthetic results. In vain do we march with unprecedented strides to empire so colossal, outvying the antique, beyond Alexander's, beyond the proudest sway of Rome. In vain have we annex'd Texas, California, Alaska, and reach north for Canada and south for Cuba. It is as if we were somehow being endow'd with a vast and more and more thoroughly-appointed body, and then left with little or no soul.

1. What point about American culture does Whitman make through his reference to the magician's snake?
   _____
   _____

2. What tone does Whitman create through phrases such as "fashionably dress'd speculators and vulgarians" and "uplifting the masses out of their sloughs"?
   _____
   _____

3. According to Whitman, how is American democracy both a success and a failure?
   _____
   _____

4. What bias about society is expressed in this excerpt?
   _____
   _____

World History   Skill Reinforcement Activities   23

Name _____ Date _____ Class _____

 **SKILL REINFORCEMENT** Activity **24**

Using E-Mail

You can use a computer to communicate directly with another computer user through E-mail, or electronic mail. Although many E-mail programs offer a variety of features, most allow you to perform these basic functions: composing and sending messages, responding to an incoming message, forwarding a message, organizing E-mail into folders, and saving and deleting messages. Become familiar with an E-mail system by sending an E-mail message to yourself. Then answer the questions that follow.

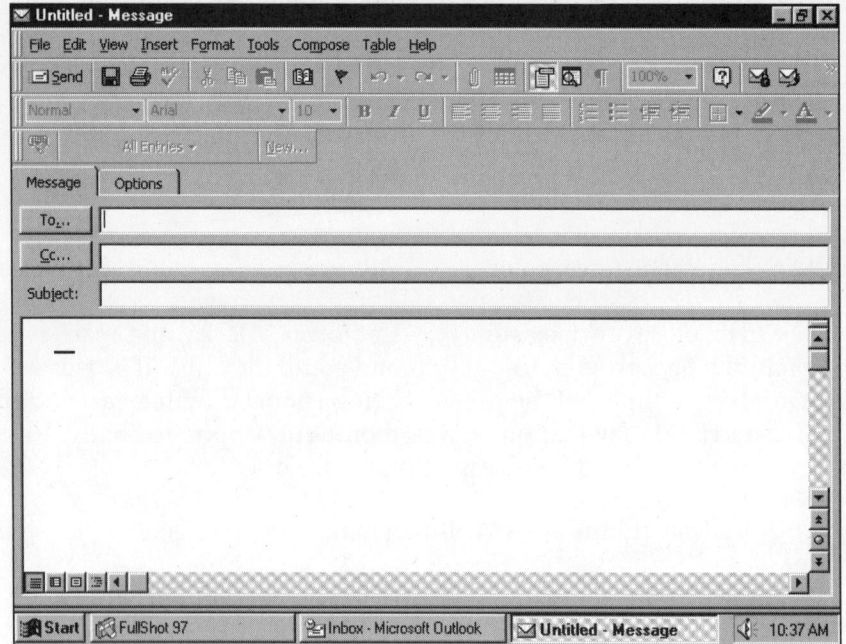

1. What do you enter in the "To" portion of the message header? _____
   _____

2. How do you move the cursor to the "Subject" text box? _____
   _____

3. Why is it unnecessary to identify yourself in the body of your message? _____
   _____

4. How do you send your message? _____
   _____

5. Check the message you sent by looking in your "In" mailbox. What information was automatically supplied in the header portion?
   _____
   _____

24   Skill Reinforcement Activities   *World History*

Name _____ Date _____ Class _____

SKILL REINFORCEMENT Activity 25

Reading a Cartogram

Although the size and shape of a country in a cartogram may have little resemblance to the country's actual physical geography, the information presented in a cartogram allows you to make comparisons between countries. Review the cartogram below, then use it to answer the questions that follow.

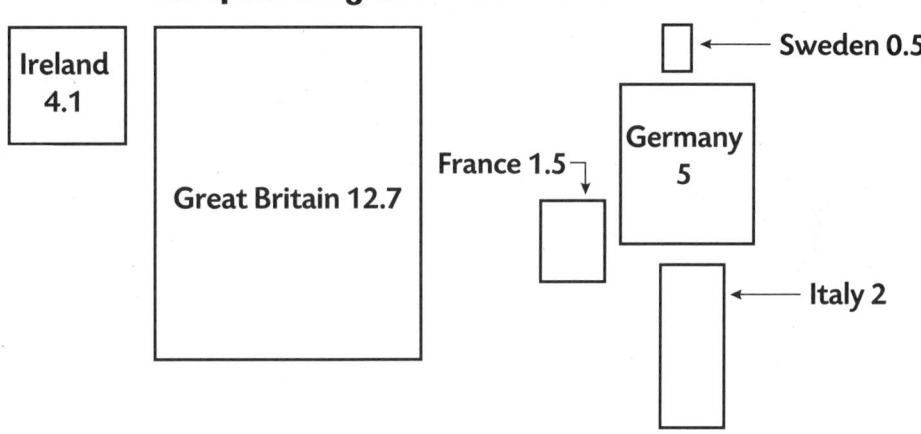

European Emigration 1821–1910

(Numbers represent millions of people.)

1. Which country had the most emigrants?
   _____

2. Which country had the fewest emigrants?
   _____

3. Which countries lost fewer than 3 million emigrants?
   _____

4. Which countries lost more than 3 million emigrants?
   _____

5. What is the relationship between the size of the country as represented on the cartogram and its number of emigrants?
   _____
   _____

6. Compare this cartogram with the map of European emigration on page 673 of your textbook. What advantage(s) does the cartogram have? What advantage(s) does the historical map have?
   _____
   _____

World History   Skill Reinforcement Activities   **25**

Name .... Date .... Class ....

SKILL REINFORCEMENT Activity 26

Selecting and Using Research Sources

Knowing what kinds of research sources to use when you are looking for information on different types of subjects can help you find what you need more quickly. Review the brief descriptions of research materials below. Then decide which source you would use to answer each of the following questions. Write the letter of the best resource in the blank. Then complete the activity that follows.

---

a. ENCYCLOPEDIA: set of books with short articles on many subjects

b. ATLAS: collection of maps and charts with an alphabetical index

c. ALMANAC: collection of current statistics and facts that is updated annually

d. BIOGRAPHICAL DICTIONARY: short biographies listed alphabetically

e. CATALOG: computer or card listing of all of a library's materials; can be searched by subject, author, or title

f. PERIODICAL GUIDE: print or computer listing of magazine articles; can be searched by subject, author, or title

---

____ **1.** What are the cultural differences among the Balkan states?

____ **2.** What are the borders of Austria today?

____ **3.** What was the court of Nicholas II and Alexandra like?

____ **4.** What do present-day historians think about the accomplishments of Otto von Bismarck?

____ **5.** What did Giuseppe Garibaldi do while he was in the United States?

____ **6.** What are the major industries of Russia, Germany, Italy, and Austria today?

____ **7.** Suppose you are doing a summer internship at your local public television station. Your boss asks you to start collecting information on turn-of-the-century Vienna for a special series that is being developed. The six-part series will feature the people, events, art, and music of Vienna 100 years ago as well as a look at life in Vienna today. Using your school or local library, list below at least three specific books or articles you would use to find the information you need. Include more than one type of research source. After each source, explain what kind of information it would provide for the television series.

_____

_____

_____

_____

_____

26   Skill Reinforcement Activities   World History

Name _____ Date _____ Class _____

SKILL REINFORCEMENT Activity 27

Using the Internet

List-based search engines, such as Yahoo, organize Web sites into general categories. Once you find the right category, you can see a list of all Web sites in that category. Keyword-oriented search engines, such as Alta Vista, Excite, and WebCrawler, are organized like gigantic indexes and are good for finding information on a specific topic.

Use two search engines to find the answers to the questions below. Record the information requested.

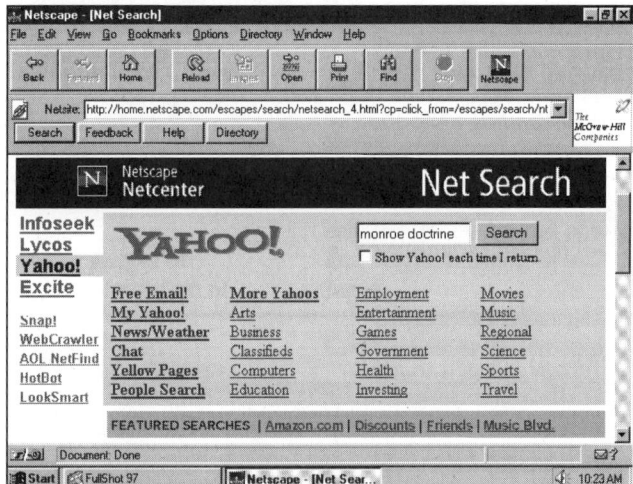

1. **a.** What is the Monroe Doctrine? _____
   b. Search engines tried: _____
   c. Search words entered or links followed: _____
   d. The URL of a Web page with helpful information: _____

2. **a.** How was the Monroe Doctrine interpreted and applied by United States Presidents?
   _____
   b. Search engines tried: _____
   c. Search words entered or links followed: _____
   _____
   d. The URL of a Web page with helpful information: _____

3. **a.** What role did the Monroe Doctrine play in the twentieth century?
   _____
   b. Search engines tried: _____
   c. Search words entered or links followed: _____
   _____
   d. The URL of a Web page with helpful information: _____

World History   Skill Reinforcement Activities   27

Name .... Date .... Class ....

SKILL REINFORCEMENT Activity 28

Interpreting Military Movements on Maps

When looking at a map that explains military information such as battles, troop movements, and conquered territory, it is important to read the map key. The key tells you what various colors and symbols on the map represent. Study the key to the map below, then use the map to answer the questions that follow.

1. **a.** Before the war began, to what country did Warsaw belong? _____

   b. Was Finland part of Russia after World War I? _____

   c. Judging from the map, which was bigger, the Russian Empire or the Soviet Union? _____

2. **a.** The White Russian armies attacked from which two main directions?
   _____
   _____

   b. Who commanded these armies?
   _____

3. Which two of the following were not controlled by the Communists at the end of 1917: Moscow, Petrograd, Kharkov, Kiev, Minsk? _____

4. Which troops invaded from the city of Murmansk?
   _____

5. The French fleet attacked which cities in the south?
   _____

6. Which anti-Bolshevik army attacked the city of Minsk? _____

7. Which groups made up the Entente fleet arriving at Archangel?
   _____

28   Skill Reinforcement Activities   World History

Name .... Date .... Class ....

SKILL REINFORCEMENT Activity 29

Analyzing Political Cartoons

Political cartoons are a type of drawing that can be used to present editorial opinions, comment on social change, criticize current events, and point out political situations. Political cartoonists use different techniques to achieve their aims. These methods include: caricature, exaggerating a person's distinctive features; size distortion, making specific people or objects larger or smaller; symbols, using people, places, or objects to represent abstract ideas; and captions, placing words or sentences under the cartoon.

The political cartoon below comments on communism. Study the political cartoon, and answer the questions below.

The Red Peril

Frank & Marie-Therese Wood Print Collections, Alexandria, VA

1. What does the fire represent?
_____

2. Why do you think the symbol of fire was chosen?
_____

3. What is the fire endangering?
_____
_____

4. What is the message of the cartoon?
_____
_____
_____

World History — Skill Reinforcement Activities

Name _____ Date _____ Class _____

SKILL REINFORCEMENT
Activity 30

Identifying an Argument

An argument is the presentation of an opinion. The main idea, or thesis, of an argument is the writer's or speaker's basic position or viewpoint. In some arguments, the thesis is stated. In others, you must read carefully to determine the writer's position. Read the statement below by Kemal Atatürk to his people, and review the discussion of Turkey in Section 1 of your textbook, pages 796–797. Then answer the following questions.

"You will be lepers, pariahs, alone in your obstinacy, with your customs of another age. Remain yourselves, but learn how to take from the West what is indispensable to an evolved people."

1. What is Atatürk's thesis in this quotation?
_____
_____

2. What reasons does Atatürk give to support this thesis?
_____
_____

3. What is Atatürk's bias in this statement?
_____
_____

4. What actions did Atatürk take that reflected his belief in this statement?
_____
_____

5. Look at a biography of a leader of a country in Asia, Africa, or Latin America between 1919 and 1939. Find a quotation from that person that states an argument about a political or historical issue. Identify the thesis of the argument and major reasons and evidence supporting it. Decide whether you accept or reject this argument, and explain why.
_____
_____
_____
_____
_____
_____
_____

30   Skill Reinforcement Activities   World History

Name _____ Date _____ Class _____

SKILL REINFORCEMENT Activity 31

Synthesizing Information

When you synthesize information, you combine information you have obtained from several sources. In doing research, you should not rely on only one source. It is better to find a variety of sources, even ones that show opposing points of view, in order to see all sides of an issue. Read the two excerpts below regarding the use of the atomic bomb by the United States in 1945. Then answer the questions that follow.

From the Interim Committee on Military Use of the Atomic Bomb, 1945

It was pointed out that one atomic bomb on an arsenal would not be much different from the effect caused by any Air Corps strike of present dimensions. However, *Dr. Oppenheimer* stated that the visual effect of an atomic bombing would be tremendous. It would be accompanied by a brilliant luminescence which would rise to a height of 10,000 to 20,000 feet. The neutron effect of the explosion would be dangerous to life for a radius of at least two-thirds of a mile.

After much discussion concerning various types of targets and the effects to be produced, *the Secretary expressed the conclusion, on which there was general agreement, that we could not give the Japanese any warning; that we could not concentrate on a civilian area; but that we should seek to make a profound psychological impression on as many of the inhabitants as possible. At the suggestion of Dr. Conant the Secretary agreed that the most desirable target would be a vital war plant employing a large number of workers and closely surrounded by workers' houses.*

From the Franck Committee on a Noncombat Atomic Demonstration, 1945

Thus, from the "optimistic" point of view—looking forward to an international agreement on prevention of nuclear warfare—the military advantages and the saving of American lives, achieved by the sudden use of atomic bombs against Japan, may be outweighed by the ensuing loss of confidence and wave of horror and repulsion, sweeping over the rest of the world, and perhaps dividing even the public opinion at home.

From this point of view a demonstration of the new weapon may best be made before the eyes of representatives of all United Nations, on the desert or a barren island. The best possible atmosphere for the achievement of an international agreement could be achieved if America would be able to say to the world, "You see what weapon we had but did not use. We are ready to renounce its use in the future and to join other nations in working out adequate supervision of the use of this nuclear weapon."

1. What conclusion was reached by the Interim Committee on Military Use of the Atomic Bomb?
_____

2. What conclusion was reached by the Franck Committee on a Noncombat Atomic Demonstration?
_____

3. What goals were being considered in the discussion of why to use the bomb?
_____

4. Compare the ways the effects of the atomic bomb are characterized in the two excerpts.
_____

5. By synthesizing the two sources, what conclusions can you draw about the decision to use atomic bombs against Japan?
_____

World History   Skill Reinforcement Activities

Name _____ Date _____ Class _____

SKILL REINFORCEMENT
Activity 32

Understanding World Time Zones

Before 1800, people set their clocks by the sun. People lived by local time, and local times varied widely. Then, in 1884, an international conference established the Prime Meridian and the International Date Line in order to standardize time zones around the world. Read the scenario below about a fictitious journey to Nepal. Then use the directions and map on page 891 of your textbook to answer the questions that follow.

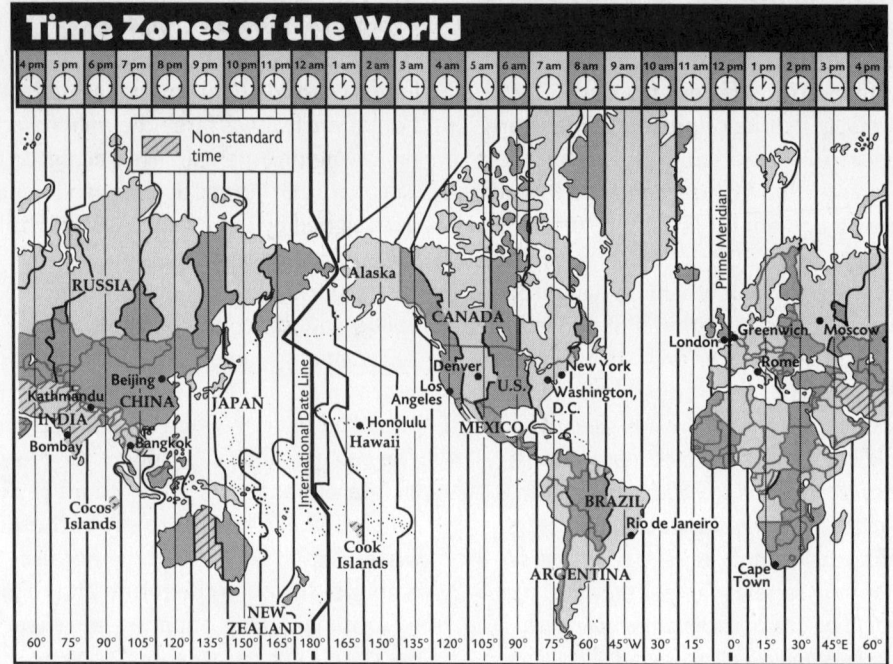

Imagine that you are going to follow in the footsteps of Edmund Hillary and Tenzing Norgay by hiking to Kala Pattar ("black rock"), the world's best vantage point for viewing Mt. Everest. You will travel by airplane from your home in Denver, Colorado, to Kathmandu, the capital of Nepal.

1. You leave Denver at 10:30 a.m., Monday, May 24, on a 2.5-hour flight to Los Angeles. What time is it in Los Angeles when you arrive? _____ What time is it in Denver? _____

2. From Los Angeles, you take a 19-hour flight across the Pacific Ocean to Bangkok. Your plane departs at 1:00 p.m. on Friday, May 24. What date and time is it in Bangkok when the flight arrives? _____ What date and time is it in Denver? _____

3. When you change planes in Bangkok, how many time zones away from Denver are you? _____ How many time zones away from Kathmandu are you? _____

32 Skill Reinforcement Activities World History

Name _____ Date _____ Class _____

SKILL REINFORCEMENT Activity 33

Using a Spreadsheet

An electronic spreadsheet is the automated version of an accountant's ledger. It stores, manipulates, and displays numerical data. You can correct data, update data, and perform calculations.

At the end of World War II, Japan's economy was in ruins. U.S. General Douglas A. MacArthur, the Supreme Command of the Allied Powers (SCAP), however, took steps to rebuild the country. The Japanese economy expanded quickly and began to enjoy a favorable balance of trade. Use the information in the table to the right to create a spreadsheet.

Japan's Value of Exports and Imports, 1991–1996 (In billions of dollars)

Year	Exports	Imports
1991	287	235
1992	315	237
1993	340	234
1994	362	242
1995	397	276
1996	443	336

1. Enter the data from the table in the spreadsheet below.

2. Which cell shows Japan's imports in 1994?
   _____

3. Which cell shows Japan's exports in 1994?
   _____

4. Enter a formula in the appropriate cells for calculating the balance of trade in each year.

5. Based on the information in the spreadsheet, was the balance of trade in Japan from 1991–1996 favorable or unfavorable. Explain your answer.
   _____

	A	B	C	D	E	F	G	H
1		1991	1992	1993	1994	1995	1996	
2	Exports							
3	Imports							
4	Balance of Trade							

World History   Skill Reinforcement Activities **33**

Name _____ Date _____ Class _____

SKILL REINFORCEMENT Activity 34

Writing a Research Report

Because writing a research report is a complex task involving many steps, it requires careful planning. When you are planning your report, don't forget to consider the element of time. You have been given a due date, and the time you spend on each stage of your project must be adjusted to fit within your time frame. Answer the questions below. Then create a schedule for an assigned project by filling out the chart.

1. How much time do I have to complete the entire project? How much time can I spend on it each day? _____

2. Which stage of the project will probably take the most time? (Write "most time" beside one stage and "least time" beside another.)

    research _____ writing _____ revising _____

3. How much time can I dedicate to each stage?

    research _____ writing _____ revising _____

Due date of paper: _____

Task	Estimated Date for Completion	Actual Date Completed
1. Choose a general topic that interests you.		
2. Do preliminary research to explore your topic.		
3. Focus on a more narrow topic.		
4. Start to assemble a bibliography of sources.		
5. Make note cards of important quotes or information.		
6. Develop a tentative thesis for your paper.		
7. Complete your bibliography of sources.		
8. Complete your note cards.		
9. Finalize your thesis statement.		
10. Make an outline for your paper.		
11. Write a rough draft.		
12. Revise your draft (more than once, if necessary).		
13. Finish your final draft.		

34 Skill Reinforcement Activities World History

Name .... Date .... Class ....

SKILL REINFORCEMENT Activity 35

Preparing a Bibliography

A bibliography is a list of the sources used in a book or report. It can help people who read the book or report obtain more information if they want it. A bibliography also helps readers assess the value of the written material by telling them where the author got his or her information. For convenience, a bibliography follows a certain format. Books listed in a bibliography should follow this format: Author's last name, first name. <u>Full Title</u>. Place of publication: Publisher, copyright date. The title of the book should be underlined. Look at the bibliography below, and then complete the activities that follow.

Abodaher, David J. <u>Youth in the Middle East: Voices of Despair</u>. New York: Franklin Watts, 1990.

Bickerton, Ian J., and Carla L. Klausner. <u>A Concise History of the Arab-Israeli Conflict</u>. Englewood, NJ: 1991.

Ferber, Elizabeth. <u>Yasir Arafat: A Life of War and Peace</u>. Brookfield, CT: The Millbrook Press, 1995.

Tessler, Mark. A History of the Israeli-Palestinian Conflict. Bloomington, IN: Indiana University Press, 1994.

---

1. Which book in this bibliography was published most recently?
   _____

2. Which book would you choose to learn about the perspective of teenagers in the Middle East?
   _____

3. What information is missing from the second entry?
   _____

4. What error in format does the fourth entry contain?
   _____

5. Prepare a bibliography on Arab Americans. Use the library card catalog or computer listings to find the names of at least three books on this topic. Then list the books in the correct format.
   _____
   _____
   _____
   _____
   _____
   _____

World History Skill Reinforcement Activities

Name .... Date .... Class ....

SKILL REINFORCEMENT Activity 36

Developing a Database

A large amount of information can be managed and organized with the help of a computerized database program. Once you enter data in a database table, you can quickly locate a record according to key information. If you have a newspaper delivery route, for example, you could have the program list all your customers that live on a particular street. You could also locate all customers who receive newspapers on weekends only.

Research and use the information about events in Mexico from 1945 to the present. Use your text to complete the database table below by filling in the year, key event or events, and the president of Mexico at the time of the event.

Year	Event	President

36 Skill Reinforcement Activities

World History

SKILL REINFORCEMENT Activity 37

Interpreting Statistics

Differentiating between relevant and irrelevant factors to explain a given set of statistics is an important part of interpreting statistics accurately. On pages 998 and 999, you read about the decisions President Ronald Reagan made that prevented him from keeping his campaign promise to reduce the federal budget deficit. Study the chart below, which shows deficits and expenditures in the federal budget from 1980, when Reagan was elected, to 1990. Then read the list of events below the chart. Decide if each event is relevant or irrelevant to understanding the budget deficit. Explain your answers.

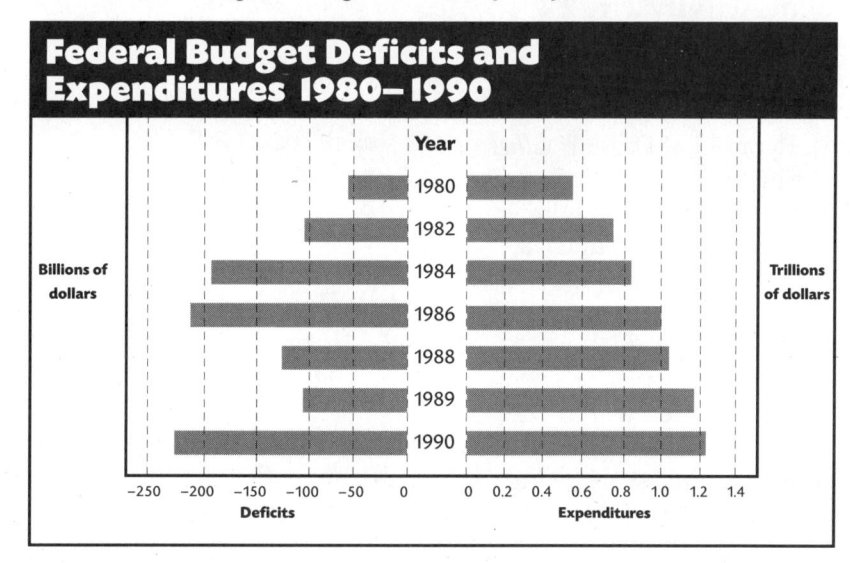

Federal Budget Deficits and Expenditures 1980–1990

Billions of dollars / Trillions of dollars

Deficits axis: −250, −200, −150, −100, −50, 0
Expenditures axis: 0, 0.2, 0.4, 0.6, 0.8, 1.0, 1.2, 1.4

Years shown: 1980, 1982, 1984, 1986, 1988, 1989, 1990

1. Massive tax cuts proposed by President Reagan and approved, with modifications, by Congress in 1981 and reductions in programs such as school lunches, student loans, and urban mass transit were offset by the largest military expansion in U.S. peacetime history.

2. In the mid-1980s Mikhail Gorbachev indicated to Reagan a willingness to negotiate arms-reduction agreements.

3. Federal spending for health care, in the form of Medicare and Medicaid payments, mounted during the Bush administration.

4. In 1985 the rock concert "Live Aid" raised $70 million for starving people in Africa.

5. Nearly 600 savings and loan associations failed in 1988–1990. The Bush administration set up a program through which the federal government would repay depositors for their losses.

World History   Skill Reinforcement Activities   37

ANSWERS

Skill Reinforcement Activity 1, p. 1
1. South America
2. The globe; it accurately shows South America as being larger than Greenland, whereas the Cylindrical Projection map distorts the size of the land areas, making Greenland seem larger.
3. Cylindrical Projection maps accurately depict the shapes of land and water and give true directions.

Skill Reinforcement Activity 2, p. 2
Djoser—Building: Step Pyramid; *Other Accomplishments:* effective bureaucracy; first stone structure
Snefru—Building: Pyramid at Dashur; *Other Accomplishments:* warrior in Nubia, Libya, and Sinai; prosperity through business and mining
Cheops—Building: Great Pyramid at Giza; *Other Accomplishments:* skilled bureaucracy

Skill Reinforcement Activity 3, p. 3
Answers will vary. Possible answers:
Identify the Problem: continued warfare in Israel
Gather Information: continued warfare in region; Saul was popular with the Israelites; David fought Goliath on Saul's behalf.
List the Options: The 12 tribes could remain without a central leader; The 12 tribes could unite under a central leader.
List the Advantages & Disadvantages: Without a central leader the Israelites were vulnerable to conquest by other peoples; United under a king, or central leader, the Israelites could build a strong government and extend the kingdom's borders.
Choose a Solution: The Israelites chose to unite under one king.

Skill Reinforcement Activity 4, p. 4
Answers will vary. Possible answers:
Unique Aspects of Egyptian Religion: not a unified system of belief; Ra, the sun god, was the most popular; some gods and goddesses had animal heads; the spirit was judged after death; had a concept of what heaven would be like; the "evil" soul wanders all over the world

Unique Aspects of Greek Religion: a well-established system of belief; deities were presented as totally human; gods were subjected to fate or necessity; souls could depart to a shadowy world called Hades; the soul could remain near the grave
Common Aspects of Egyptian and Greek Religions: worship of local deities; deities had human bodies; a spirit or soul lived on after death; this soul remaining on earth will be hungry

Skill Reinforcement Activity 5, p. 5
1. a. 37.1°N, 22.2°E
   b. 40.6°N, 22.8°E
   c. 38°N, 23.6°E
2. a. Pátrai
   b. Vólos
   c. Kérkira

Skill Reinforcement Activity 6, p. 6
1. *Alternative:* leave when the Tarquins did. *Consequences:* Roman art and architecture would have developed differently; empire less prosperous without Etruscan artisans.
2. *Alternative:* Augustus's refusal to reform. *Consequences:* lack of Roman prosperity, exploitation of provinces by officials; widespread hunger; poor roads.
3. *Alternative:* allow landowners to gain more land and slaves. *Consequences:* farmers deprived of land and business would have migrated to overcrowded cities; decline of urban living conditions; a new middle class might not have arisen in Rome.
4. *Alternative:* maintain army's existing size or increase its size. *Consequence:* larger or a status quo army might have halted or lessened invasions by outsiders.
5. *Alternative:* not build aqueducts. *Consequence:* lack of water for drinking, bathing, and farming.
6. *Alternative:* allow orderly transition of power. *Consequence:* corrupt emperors might have reigned for long periods, continuing to bankrupt treasury and further weaken the empire.

7. *Alternative:* honor the Roman emperor. *Consequence:* end of persecutions but weakening of Christianity's unique appeal to converts.
8. *Alternative:* Christianity would not have enjoyed protection. *Consequences:* persecution might have continued; Christianity would developed alongside other religions without state support.
9. *Alternative:* accept pope's authority. *Consequence:* rift between churches would not have been as abrupt or would not have occurred, but Eastern Orthodoxy's rich traditions might not have developed.
10. *Alternative:* dominance of Germanic languages. *Consequence:* classical heritage might have been lost or minimized.

Skill Reinforcement Activity 7, p. 7

1. East African trade in Roman times
2. The author is a Greek from the Roman Empire. His purpose in writing the book was to give sailors of the Roman Empire detailed information that they would need in order to compete with the Arab's trade monopoly in East Africa.
3. *catch them in a peculiar way, in wicker baskets; along this coast live men of piratical habits, very great in stature; savages*
4. The excerpt and the textbook describe the same types of goods for trade in East Africa. Both describe the African chieftains and the intermarriage of Arabs and Africans. The textbook, however, does not use the emotionally charged words and phrases to describe the East Africans.

Skill Reinforcement Activity 8, p. 8

Match 1 with 6, 2 with 7, 3 with 5, 4 with 8.

Skill Reinforcement Activity 9, p. 9

1. Liu wants to convince the Chinese people to obey him so that he can remain the leader of China. He uses examples of Qin abuses, as well as his planned improvements, to convince people that Han rule would be better for them.
2. *Answers may include peasants, merchants, lords, scholars, or civil servants.*
3. Qin laws were harsh and resulted in the deaths of many people, from peasants to scholars.
4. The *Pax Sinica*, 400 years of peace and stability under Han emperors who were descendants of Liu, indicates that Liu's promises were kept.
5. *Students should give well-reasoned responses using concrete events mentioned in the chapter that match their knowledge of what issues would be of importance to a Chinese peasant; for example, food, freedom from oppression, no forced labor.*

Skill Reinforcement Activity 10, p. 10

1. It represents an opinion. The expression "woman behind the man" implies that Theodora was responsible for her husband's success.
2. a. Justinian was well-educated. Theodora had been an actress before they were married. She gave jobs to friends. Justinian issued decrees allowing women to own land. There was a rebellion, which Justinian suppressed.
   b. They can be proved by looking in history books or an encyclopedia.
3. *surprising, generously, fair, greatest*
4. Theodora was a smart woman who was a good influence upon her husband, helping him to remain in power.

Skill Reinforcement Activity 11, p. 11

1. *Possible answer:* Projected Population Increase in the Middle East From 2000–2020
2. Iran
3. Jordan
4. 17,549,000; 96 percent
5. Egypt
6. approximately 130 million

Skill Reinforcement Activity 12, p. 12

1. *Students may infer that, by putting her at the "scene" of an important event for Christians, Christianity itself is important to her.*
2. *Students may infer that the apes are questioning the role of the wise men and, by extension, men in positions of authority.*
3. *Students may infer that the ape-angel is questioning the authority of God and the Church because it is about to "unravel" the word of God.*
4. *Students may infer again that a certain questioning is going on—perhaps of worldly rule or riches—or they may infer that the images are purely for entertainment.*

Skill Reinforcement Activity 13, p. 13
1. A.D. 1095, A.D. 1147, A.D. 1189, A.D. 1204
2. Third Crusade; from London, England; passed through Marseilles, Genoa, Tyre, Acre
3. all of Europe except southern and eastern Spain, Russia, part of Turkey
4. north Africa, part of Spain, the Middle East

Skill Reinforcement Activity 14, p. 14
1. *Answers will vary, but may include:* Harmony is the glue binding society together; Buddhist laws and codes should be worshiped by all; only a minority of people are smart, most are easily influenced.
2. *Answers will vary but may include:* Following Confucian and Buddhist beliefs will lead to unlimited progress in human affairs; without a universally accepted moral code, human society will degenerate into petty partisan squabbling.
3. *Quotes should be appropriately referenced to the generalization to which they belong.*

Skill Reinforcement Activity 15, p. 15
1. Primary sources: the journal of Pedro de Castañeda, 1560; *Royal Commentaries of the Incas*, by Garcilaso de la Vega, 1600s. Secondary Sources: *Aztecs: An Interpretation* by Inga Clendinnen, 1991; *Civilizations in the West* by Mark Kishlansky, Patrick Geary, and Patricia O'Brien, 1991
2. Inga Clendinnen, Mark Kishlansky, Patrick Geary, and Patricia O'Brien are modern historians. Pedro de Castañeda was a soldier in the army of Francisco Coronado. Garcilaso de la Vega was born in Peru in 1539 of Inca and Spanish ancestry.
3. No, because it is possible that a translator may misinterpret a statement in a document or distort what the original author had in mind when he or she originally wrote the piece.

Skill Reinforcement Activity 16, p. 16
1. Evidence is offered of what the English think of themselves, their way of thinking anyone "handsome" as being English, and their questioning whether any "delicacies" exist in other countries.
2. The evidence is that the English imagine that everyone visiting their country has come to exploit the English in some way, and they don't even have friends among themselves.
3. Students may answer that the first evidence is more convincing because the author selects specific evidence directly related to the claim, whereas the second claim has evidence that is only tangentially related to it.
4. The source for the evidence appears to be things English people actually say. This is primary evidence as it is words spoken at that time and not made up after the event.
5. The evidence and the claims may not be objective but may be based on the writer's prejudice, such as dislike for the English.

Skill Reinforcement Activity 17, p. 17
1. 8 items
2. The fight against slavery (line 5)
3. line 1
4. Schomburg-Gen. Research
5. line 4
6. (Another Search)

Skill Reinforcement Activity 18, p. 18
Answers vary depending on the word-processing software program used by each student.

Skill Reinforcement Activity 19, p. 19
Appearance: "old men have grey beards, that their faces are wrinkled, their eyes purging thick amber and plum-tree gum"
Intelligence: ". . . they have a plentiful lack of wit"
Physical Strength: "the most weak hams"

Skill Reinforcement Activity 20, p. 20
Answers will vary depending on the topic, the multimedia resources available, and the student's imagination.

Skill Reinforcement Activity 21, p. 21
Students' answers may vary. Possible answers:
I. B. Paul Revere and William Dawes warn Minutemen
II. Moving Toward Separation
II. A. 2. Olive Branch Petition
II. B. 1. Written by Thomas Paine
II. C. Declaration of Independence
III. War for Independence
III. A. 1–2. Must fight a long-distance war; Must conquer entire country
III. B. American Advantages
III. B. 2. Help from French—arms and ammunition

III. C. 2. Yorktown
IV. A. Articles of Confederation
IV. A. 2–3. Government could not force states to pay national debt; Government could not regulate states' economic activity
IV. B. 1. Federal system
IV. B. 2.a–c. Executive; Legislative; Judicial
IV. C. Bill of Rights
IV. C. 2. Protected the rights of individual states

Skill Reinforcement Activity 22, p. 22

1. percentage of population and percentage of land ownership
2. a. 1 percent
   b. 10 percent
3. a. 2 percent
   b. 25 percent
4. a. 97 percent
   b. 65 percent
5. *Answers may vary, but should refer to the fundamental importance of agriculture.*
6. the Second Estate
7. a. It was the only estate whose percentage of population exceeded its percentage of land ownership.
   b. *Answers will vary, but should refer to the fundamental inequality of this situation and to the resentment it bred.*

Skill Reinforcement Activity 23, p. 23

Answers will vary. Possible answers:
1. Moneymaking has become the only goal.
2. a sarcastic, critical tone
3. American democracy is a success in producing material goods and a failure in fostering the realization of higher aims.
4. A crass society focuses on material production; a truly great society strives for distinction in moral virtue, literature, and the arts.

Skill Reinforcement Activity 24, p. 24

1. the E-mail name and address of the recipient; If the recipient is on the same network, the E-mail name is sufficient.
2. either by pressing the [TAB] button on your keyboard or by using the mouse to point and click the cursor to the Subject text box
3. because the recipient(s) will see the E-mail name of the sender before they open the message
4. by clicking on the [SEND] button located on the toolbar
5. In many programs the date, name, and address of sender are supplied automatically.

Skill Reinforcement Activity 25, p. 25

1. Great Britain
2. Sweden
3. Sweden, France, and Italy
4. Ireland, Germany, and Great Britain
5. The size of a country and the number of emigrants is directly proportional. The greater the number of emigrants, the larger the country appears on the cartogram.
6. *Possible answer:* The cartogram makes the relative numbers of emigrants immediately visible. The historical map shows the actual geographic relationships between countries and provides an accurate representation of physical geography of each country.

Skill Reinforcement Activity 26, p. 26

1. a
2. b
3. e
4. e *or* f
5. a *or* d
6. c
7. *Answers will vary, but should include at least three specific books or articles and at least two different types of research sources. Information sought in each book or article should be appropriate to the type of source.*

Skill Reinforcement Activity 27, p. 27

1–4. *Answers will vary for questions 1–4 depending on the search engine used and the information found on the Internet. General answers will relate to the Monroe Doctrine as a U.S. foreign policy principle that stated that the Americas were off-limits to European intervention. U.S. Presidents invoked the Doctrine successfully several times. During the Age of Imperialism, Latin America feared the Monroe Doctrine as a justification for the expansion of U.S. power in the region. Under Franklin D. Roosevelt, the doctrine became less important as the U.S. stressed cooperation and nonintervention. During the 1960s, the Doctrine was challenged by the Soviet Union's support for communist Cuba.*

Skill Reinforcement Activity 28, p. 28

1. **a.** the Russian Empire
   b. no
   c. the Russian Empire
2. **a.** from the south and the east
   b. Denikin and Kolchak
3. Petrograd, Kiev
4. British, French, Canadians, Italians, Serbs
5. Odessa, Simferopol
6. Polish
7. British, French, Canadians, Americans

Skill Reinforcement Activity 29, p. 29

1. Bolshevism (early name for Soviet communism)
2. Fire represents something that is destructive and on the move.
3. Houses, buildings, fields, etc. that represent a peaceful and ordered way of life.
4. People in all countries of the world should be aware that Soviet communism is a danger to their traditional values.

Skill Reinforcement Activity 30, p. 30

1. The Turks should keep their national identity but should also modernize.
2. The Turks will be rejected by the rest of the world if they do not modernize.
3. He thinks Western government and other advances are useful.
4. He encouraged Turks to develop their national identity by purifying their language, but at the same time adopted Western systems of writing, timekeeping, education, and government. He allowed women to remove their veils and ordered men to stop wearing the fez.
5. *Answers will vary. Students should be able to identify a quotation that expresses an argument and identify the main idea and reasoning of the argument.*

Skill Reinforcement Activity 31, p. 31

1. The atomic bomb should be dropped without warning on a Japanese war plant to have a strong psychological effect on the population.
2. An atomic bomb should be first demonstrated in an international arena, rather than dropped on Japan, in order to prevent negative public opinion both at home and abroad.
3. saving American lives; ending the war; and achieving an international agreement to prevent future wars
4. The first excerpt, which supports military use of the bomb, emphasizes the visual and psychological effects of the bomb but downplays the human devastation. The second excerpt, which is against military use of the bomb, refers to the "horror" and "revulsion" that dropping the bomb would bring.
5. The two excerpts show that the question of using the atomic bomb for the first time was highly controversial and went through much debate. Some felt that immediate military objectives had to prevail, while others, sensing the public response such a bomb would produce, felt that it should come under international control and not be used for military purposes.

Skill Reinforcement Activity 32, p. 32

1. 12:00 noon, 1:00 p.m.
2. Saturday, May 25, 11:00 p.m.; Saturday, May 25, 9:00 a.m.
3. 10, 2

Skill Reinforcement Activity 33, p. 33

1. Students should enter the data from the table in the spreadsheet.
2. Cell E3
3. Cell E2
4. B2–B3 for cell B4; C2–C3 for cell C4; D2–D3 for cell D4; E2–E3 for cell E4; F2–F3 for cell F4; G2–G3 for cell G4.
5. Favorable; The value of Japan's exports was greater than the value of Japan's imports for all years 1991–1996.

Skill Reinforcement Activity 34, p. 34

Answers will vary, but should take into account the time frame for the research report and the different time allotments needed for different tasks. Encourage students to use this schedule for an actual research report they have been assigned.

Skill Reinforcement Activity 35, p. 35

1. *Yasir Arafat: A Life of War and Peace*
2. *Youth in the Middle East: Voices of Despair*
3. the name of the publisher
4. The title of the book should be underlined.

5. *Student bibliographies will vary, but should include all required information and follow the correct format.*

Skill Reinforcement Activity 36, p. 36

Students should create a database of key events in the history of Mexico from 1945–present-day. Entries will vary based on the information chosen by students to include in the database. Examples of dates, events, and presidents included: 1985, Mexico City earthquake, Miguel de la Madrid Hurtado; 1993, NAFTA implemented, Carlos Salinas de Gortari; 1994, Economic crisis in Mexico, Ernesto Zedillo Ponce de Léon

Skill Reinforcement Activity 37, p. 37

1. Relevant: The growth in military spending helps explain why both expenditures and deficits increased between 1980 and 1982.
2. Irrelevant: Discussing arms reduction does not affect the budget.
3. Relevant: Expenditures and deficits increased during the Bush administration (1989–1990 on the chart).
4. Irrelevant: The $70 million came from individuals and so did not affect the country's increased expenditures.
5. Relevant: Repaying depositors cost the government large amounts of money, which increased the deficit.

ACKNOWLEDGMENTS

Text

7 From *The Periplus of the Erythraean Sea*, translated by William Schoff (New York: Longmans, Green, and Co., 1912, pp. 27–29. Reprinted by permission in *Readings in World History*, edited by Leften S. Stavrianos, et. al., copyright ©1965 by Allyn and Bacon, Inc.

9 From "The Rise of Liu Chi, Founder of the Han" from *Sources of Chinese Tradition* compiled by Wm. Theodore de Bary et. al., copyright © 1960 by Columbia University Press.

12 From *Image on the Edge: The Margins of Medieval Art* by Michael Camille, copyright © 1992 by Michael Camille.

14 From *Sources of Japanese Tradition* compiled by Ryusaku Tsunoda et. al., copyright © 1958 by Columbia University Press.

15 From *Aztecs: An Interpretation*, by Inga Clendinnen, copyright ©1991 by Cambridge University Press
From *Civilizations in the West*, by Mark Kishlansky, Patrick Geary, and Patricia O'Brien, copyright ©1991 by Harper Collins Publishers
From *Riding With Coronado*, adapted and edited by Robert Meredith and Edric B. Smith, Jr., copyright © 1964 by Edric B. Smith, Jr. and Robert K. Meredith. By permission of Little, Brown and Company.
From *Royal Commentaries of the Incas*, Part One, by Carcilaso de la Vega, El Inca, tr. by Harold V. Livermore, copyright © 1966 by University of Texas Press.

16 From *A Relation . . . of the Island of England . . . c. 1500* translated by C. A. Sneyd from *The Portable Renaissance Reader* edited by James Bruce Ross and Mary Martin McLaughlin, copyright © 1953 by the Viking Press.

19 From *Hamlet* by William Shakespeare.

23 From *Democratic Vistas* in *Complete Prose Works* by Walt Whitman, edited by Richard Maurice Burke, Thomas B. Harned, and Horace L. Traubel (New York: G.P. Putnam's Sons, 1902), II, 61–66.

30 From speech by Mustafa Kemal Pasha from *Kemal Atatürk* by Frank Tachau, copyright © 1987 by Chelsea House Publishers.

31 From "The Interim Committee on Military Use of the Atomic Bomb, 1945" and "The Franck Committee on a Noncombat Atomic Demonstration, 1945" from *Major Problems in American Foreign Policy* edited by Thomas G. Paterson, copyright © 1989 by D. C. Heath and Company.

36 *World Book Encyclopedia Yearbook*, 1992–1997

37 From *The Enduring Vision: A History of the American People, 2nd ed.* by Paul S. Boyer et. al., copyright © 1993 by D. C. Heath and Company.

Maps

Cartographic services provided by Ortelius Design, and Joe LeMonnier.

Photographs

12 By permission of The British Library, ms. no. 36684 folio 46v.

29 *The Red Peril*, by Nelson Harding, copyright © 1919, *The Brooklyn Eagle*.